The New Spiralizer Cookbook

75 Exciting Vegetable Spiralizer Recipes For Paleo, Gluten-Free, Low Carb, Dairy Free And Other Healthy Diets

PAULA COREY

ISBN-13: 978-1515045946

ISBN-10: 1515045943

DEDICATION

To all who want to live healthy and have a vibrant life.

TABLE OF CONTENTS

Read Other Books By Paula Corey:

56 Low Fat Salads, Dips And Dressings For Faster Weight Loss

Available at popular online retailers.

INTRODUCTION

Many of us love traditional pasta but a new breed of noodles is taking over our kitchen tables. Spiralized vegetables is the new "shift" in healthy eating. This book contains 75 exciting vegetable spiralizer recipes for people on paleo, gluten-free or low carb diets. Most of the recipes are also diary free and can be eaten by almost anyone who wants to cut back on carbs, eat adequate fruits and vegetables and also maintain a healthy weight.

The spiralizer is the must-have kitchen gadget for those who are conscious of the food they eat. It has always been possible to shred or slice a range of vegetables into thin ribbons using a julienne peeler. However, this technique has been greatly improved and made more appealing by this Japanese invention called spiralizer. This reasonably priced gadget will literarily transform the way you cook!

The possible uses of spiralized vegetables are endless. You can substitute most pasta dishes with spiralized vegetables. Spiralized noodles are very useful as substitute pasta in soups, salads, casseroles, chips and stir fries. You can also replace rice with "spiralized vegetable rice" to create a whole new set of dishes.

The Basics Of Using A Spiralizer

Spiralizing is simply the process of cutting vegetables into noodle spirals. These noodles are attractive to the health-conscious because they are free of preservatives, dairy free, gluten free and have a low glycemic index. Once your spiralizer has arrived, it is important to know the proper way to use it.

1

Here Is A Step By Step For Using A Hand Crank Spiralizer:

Step 1: Prepare The Vegetable

Cut the ends of the veggies before peeling to save time. It is better to choose vegetables that are as straight as possible and at least 2 inches in thickness. When you do have a curved vegetable, cut it in half to reduce the curve and then spiralize each part separately. Also veggies that are longer than 12 inches should be cut in half. Cut off the ends of the vegetable as straight as possible so it can be placed flush with the spiralizer. Peel the vegetable if necessary e.g. butternut squash.

Step Two: Properly Line Up And Secure The Vegetable

After trimming your veggies, it is important to ensure that they are properly lined up. Secure the vegetable at both ends and center it into the spikes. Press down firmly to ensure the spikes get a good grip. Center the other end of the vegetable in metal beanie. This is essential so that it does not slip off or create noodles with irregular shapes.

Securing the base of the spiralizer is also important. Secure your spiralizer on a flat surface (such as a countertop) by pressing down firmly on the suction-cup feet.

Step 3: Turn The Crank To Spiralize

Apply pressure on the handle at the bottom with one hand then use the other hand to crank the spiralizer clockwise. Your vegetable will be transformed instantly into noodles.

Choose Your Zoodle Shapes:

**The spiralizer comes with 3 blade sizes. The smallest blade creates noodles with the thickness of spaghetti (use this for Asian or Italian noodle substitutes). The larger blade creates noodles about the size of bucatini (great for curly fries). The flat blade is for ribbon spiral zoodles like pappardelle.

Cut Vegetable Noodles:

Vegetable noodles can be really long. It is best to use a knife to cut them into lengths that are manageable. You can also chop them into 1-inch pieces for rice substitutes.

Use Leftover Veggies:

When you spiralize veggies, you will have leftover ends and plugs. You can slice these and use in stocks, soups, casseroles and sautés. To make vegetable stock, keep a large resealable bag in your freezer and fill it the scraps from spiralizing and other cooking activity. Once the bag is full, dump it in a slow cooker, add salt and bay leaves, cover with water and cook on low for about 8 hours. They could also be converted to compost if you have a garden.

What You Can Spiralize

Your spiralizer will enable you to make a wide variety of dishes. These include pasta, noodles, rice, casseroles, soups, fries & chips, salads, buns and even pizza!

There are about 24 fruits and vegetables that you can spiralize. About half of the fruits/veggies on this list can also be eaten raw:

Apples

Broccoli

Beets

Butternut Squash

Carrots

Cabbage

Chayote

Celeriac

Cucumber

Daikon Radish

Dragon Fruit

Eddoe

Kohlrabi

Jicama

Onions

Parsnips

Persimmons

Pears

Plantains

Sweet Potato

Rutabaga

Turnip

Zucchini

Spiralizing Benefits

Spiralizing is beneficial to different individuals in a variety of ways. You may have health-related goals or just want to add more creativity and convenience to the kitchen. One or two of the benefits below will apply to.

Helps In Maintaining A Paleo Or Gluten Free Diet

Paleo and gluten free diets require the avoidance of products that contain wheat. Individuals who have gluten sensitivity or gluten intolerance may not be too happy about the quality of gluten-free pastry they have to eat. Your meals will become more enjoyable and exciting when you start spiralizing. You can manipulate spiralized noodles and spiralized rice in many ways to bring endless variety to your kitchen and replace wheat-based meals. Your meals will be more nutritious, food will digest easily and you won't have disruptive gastrointestinal problems.

Boosts Weight Loss And Health Goals

Spiralized vegetables add a good quantity of low carb, low calorie, low sugar and high fiber ingredients to your meals. They also help you to avoid processed food. Vegetables make you feel full and you can easily avoid overeating. This is a great way to get rid of the feeling of "starving" when you are on a diet. You can eat more and still maintain an ideal intake of calories.

Provides Foods With Low Glycemic Index

Traditional pasta and breads have high glycemic index. People with diabetes have to avoid or monitor wheat-based or starchy foods. A good way to do this is to eat low-glycemic vegetables in place of high-sugar foods. Eat spiralized veggies to avoid crashes and monitor your blood sugar levels.

Fills Your Meals With Fiber

When you spiralize often, your meals will be filled with fiber. You will enjoy constant natural bodily cleansing and detoxification. Wheat products, pasta and breads do not have much fiber. Furthermore, the fiber in spiralized vegetables are unprocessed.

Enables You To Eat Fresh Food And Vegetables Conveniently

By adding spiralized veggies to a meal, you have automatically created a nutritious dish. No longer do you have to make a side salad or put pressure on your kids to eat vegetables. Your family will eat nutritious food willingly and life will be easier for you.

Add Color And Creativity To Your Meals

With 24 or more spiralizable fruits and vegetables, you will never run out of excitement in your kitchen. Each meal can be easily transformed into a beautiful and nutritious culinary delight. You can't get this variation with pasta.

Have fun and stay healthy.

Paula Corey

ZUCCHINI RECIPES WITH MEAT, SEAFOOD OR EGGS

Easy Zucchini Noodles

Preparation: 20 minutes

Cooking Time: 0 minutes

Serves 2

Ingredients:

4 cups spiralized zucchini (about 4 small zucchini)

1/2 teaspoon salt

2 tablespoon almond meal or almond flour

1 teaspoon coconut oil

2 garlic cloves, crushed

2 tablespoons of extra-virgin olive oil

5 eggs, scrambled

7

Salt and pepper, to taste

Directions:

1. Add zucchini noodles to a wire strainer or colander. Add salt liberally and toss to coat. Set aside for 20 minutes to drain. After 20 minutes, rinse well and use paper towels to pat dry.

2. Meanwhile, place a large skillet on medium-high heat. In a bowl, stir together almond flour, coconut oil and a sprinkle of salt. Sauté mixture in the heated skillet, stirring constantly with a wooden spoon for about 1 minute until brown. Remove the mixture from skillet and set aside.

3. Return the skillet to heat and add spiralized zucchini. Sauté for about 1-2 minutes or until just tender. Push zucchini noodles to one side of the pan, reduce to medium low heat then wait for 1 minute for the pan to cool down.

4. Add garlic and olive oil, wait for 20 seconds then pour in eggs. Allow eggs to cook until just starting to set. Gently stir zucchini noodles with eggs. Continue stirring until egg is set. Add salt and pepper to taste.

5. Serve zucchini noodles in bowls and garnish with almond flour crumbs.

Paleo Pasta Carbonara

Preparation: 15 minutes

Cooking Time: 40 minutes

Serves 4-6

Ingredients

1 medium spaghetti squash

3/4 pound of nitrate-free bacon

1 tablespoon of arrowroot powder

6 eggs

1/2 cup of full-fat coconut milk

1 teaspoon dried oregano

1 teaspoon dried basil

1 teaspoon dried parsley

1 teaspoon dried marjoram

1/4 teaspoon garlic powder

1 teaspoon kosher salt

1 tablespoon fresh Italian parsley, chopped

1 tablespoon lard

Directions:

1. Slice spaghetti squash in half and scoop out all the seeds. Place on a plate, open side down. Microwave for 10 minutes.

2. Meanwhile, fry bacon strips until crispy in a cast iron skillet over medium heat. Set bacon aside on a plate.

3. Whisk arrowroot powder with the bacon grease in the pan and cook for a few minutes over medium heat. In a bowl, stir together the eggs and the remaining ingredients (except lard) until fully incorporated. Pour egg mixture into the pan and cook with constant stirring (about 3 minutes) until cooked through but still wet.

4. Slice bacon into 1/4" strips, place in serving bowl then top with the egg mixture.

5. Scoop spaghetti squash noodles into the serving bowl then top with lard.

6. Slowly stir lard into the spaghetti squash until melted then stir together all the ingredients.

Slow Cooker Zoodle Soup

Preparation: 30 minutes

Cooking Time: 6 hours

Serves 12

Ingredients:

1 medium zucchini, spiralized

4 cups beef stock

2 ribs celery, chopped

1 carrot, chopped

1 small onion, diced

1 medium tomato, diced

1 1/2 teaspoon garlic salt

1 1/2 pound ground beef

6 garlic cloves, minced

1/2 cup nutritional yeast

1 egg

1 teaspoon dried oregano

1 teaspoon Italian seasoning

1 1/2 teaspoon onion powder

1 1/2 teaspoon sea salt

1/2 teaspoon black pepper

4 tablespoons fresh parsley, chopped

Directions:

1. Heat a large slow cooker on low.

2. Add zucchini, beef stock, celery, carrot, onion, tomato and garlic salt to the slow cooker and cover.

3. In a large bowl, mix together ground beef, garlic, nutritional yeast, egg, oregano, Italian seasoning, onion powder, sea salt, black pepper and parsley. Form the mixture into about 30 meatballs.

4. Add olive oil to a large skillet on medium-high heat. Brown meatballs in hot oil on all sides.

5. Add meatballs to the slow cooker, then cover and cook for 6 hours.

Paleo Spaghetti And Meatballs

Preparation: 20 minutes

Cooking Time: 25 minutes

Serves 4-5

Ingredients:

For Meatballs-

2 pounds ground beef

1/4 cup fresh oregano, chopped

1/4 teaspoon salt

For Spaghetti-

3 pounds zucchini, spiralized

1 tablespoon salt (for salting the zucchini)

5-6 slices thick cut bacon

8-10 ounces sliced mushrooms

12-16 fresh garlic cloves, minced

1 cup sliced black olives

3/4 cup fresh basil, chopped

Directions:

To Make meatballs-

1. Preheat oven to 400F then line a baking sheet with parchment paper or foil.

2. Use your hands to combine ground beef, oregano and salt thoroughly. Form into about 24 meatballs.

3. Bake in preheated oven for about 12-15 minutes.

To Make Spaghetti-

4. Add zucchini noodles to a wire strainer or colander. Add salt liberally and toss to coat. Set aside for 30 minutes to drain. After 30 minutes, rinse well and use paper towels to pat dry.

5. Slice bacon to small pieces. Place a large skillet on medium high heat and cook bacon with occasional stirring for about 7-8 minutes or until brown.

6. Add mushrooms and garlic and cook for 6-8 minutes more until mushrooms start to brown.

7. Add zucchini noodles and olives. Stir and cook for about 4-5 minutes or until zucchini is al dente. Add basil then cook for 1 minute more.

Serve with meatballs.

Paleo Chicken Pad Thai With Vegetable Noodles

Preparation: 20 minutes

Cooking Time: 18 minutes

Serves 3

Ingredients:

1 1/2 pound chicken breast, cut into bite size pieces

5 tablespoons extra virgin coconut oil

5 garlic cloves, chopped finely

4 tablespoon fish sauce

1/2 tablespoon apple cider vinegar

4 tablespoon fresh lime juice

2 medium carrots, julienned

1 12-ounce package of broccoli slaw

4 green onions, chopped finely

5 tablespoon chopped fresh cilantro

Directions:

1. Add oil to a wok on medium-high heat. Add garlic and cook for 1 minute.

2. Add chicken and then cook for 2-3 minutes, frequently stirring until lightly browned.

3. Next add fish sauce, vinegar and lime juice. Let simmer rapidly for about 5-8 minutes.

4. Add julienned carrot and broccoli slaw. Cook with frequent stirring for about 3-4 minutes or until soft but still firm.

5. Garnish with cilantro and green onions.

Chicken Zoodle Soup

Preparation: 15 minutes

Cooking Time: 30 minutes

Serves 4

Ingredients:

4 cups chicken stock

1 large carrot, diced

1 rib celery, diced

1 small zucchini, spiralized

Directions:

1. In a medium pot, add chicken stock and bring to a boil.

2. Turn the heat down to a simmer then add the carrots and celery. Let simmer for about 10-20 minutes or until vegetables are tender.

3. Add zucchini noodles then cook for 4-5 minutes more. Serve.

Chicken Zucchini Noodles And Basil Avocado Sauce

Preparation: 20 minutes

Cooking Time: 10 minutes

Serves 4

Ingredients:

3 cups zucchini noodles

1 cup cooked or grilled chicken, chopped

2 tablespoon extra virgin olive oil

2 garlic cloves, crushed

2 tablespoon lemon juice

1 large avocado, pitted

1 large handful of fresh basil, (plus extra for garnish)

Salt and pepper, to taste

Directions:

1. Add zucchini noodles to a wire strainer or colander. Add salt liberally and toss to coat. Set aside for 20 minutes to drain. After 20 minutes, rinse well, use paper towels to pat dry then set aside.

2. In a food processor, combine olive oil, garlic, lemon juice, avocado and basil. Blend until smooth then add salt and pepper to taste.

3. Place a saucepan on low heat. Add zucchini noodles and the avocado sauce. Add a little water if the sauce is too thick. Add chicken, stir everything together and cook until heated through. Serve immediately, garnished with basil.

Meaty Bacon Zucchini Pasta

Preparation: 20 minutes

Cooking Time: 15 minutes

Serves 4-5

Ingredients:

1 pound cooked chicken or steak, cut into bite size pieces

4 large zucchini, spiralized

1 cup bacon grease

2 garlic cloves, crushed

1/4 cup chopped fresh basil

Directions:

1. Add zucchini noodles to a wire strainer or colander. Add salt liberally and toss to coat. Set aside for 20 minutes to drain. After 20 minutes, rinse well, use paper towels to pat dry then set aside.

2. Add bacon grease to a large skillet on medium-high heat. Add the meat and cook for 3-4 minutes. Add zucchini and garlic then sauté with frequent stirring for about 4-5 minutes or until zucchini is al dente.

3. Stir in basil and cook for 2 minutes more, stirring occasionally. Serve immediately.

Paleo Zoodle Chow Mein

Preparation: 20 minutes

Cooking Time: 30 minutes

Serves 4

Ingredients:

1/2 pound chicken, cut into bite size pieces

1/2 tablespoon ghee

1 tablespoon rice vinegar

1 tablespoon coconut aminos

1 large carrot, shredded

1 small crown of broccoli, stem removed, cut into bite sized pieces

1/2 green cabbage, cored, sliced thinly

2 zucchini, spiralized

For Sauce-

3 tablespoon coconut aminos

2 tablespoon rice vinegar

1 teaspoon sesame oil

1 tablespoon fish sauce

2-inch fresh ginger, minced

2 garlic cloves, minced

1 teaspoon honey

Directions:

1. To a large wok on medium-high heat, add ghee allow to melt. Add chicken, 1 tablespoon rice vinegar and 1 tablespoon coconut aminos. Cook for 5-7 minutes with occasional stirring.

2. Whisk together all the ingredients for the sauce and add to the wok.

3. Toss carrot, broccoli and cabbage into the work. Cover then cook for about 10-15 minutes or until cabbage is soft.

4. Add zucchini noodles and then cook for 7-8 minutes more.

Zoodles With Roasted Tomatoes, Avocado And Bacon

Preparation: 10 minutes

Cooking Time: 20 minutes

Serves 4

Ingredients:

3 medium zucchini squash, spiralized

6 strips bacon, cut into 1-inch pieces

1/4 cup fresh basil leaves

1 pint cherry tomatoes

1 tablespoon lard, melted

Salt and pepper to taste

1 ripe avocado

Directions:

1. Combine bacon, tomatoes, basil and lard on a baking sheet. Season with pepper then bake for 20 minutes at 350F.

2. Meanwhile, add water and salt to a large pot. Bring to boil over high heat then add zucchini noodles. Let the zucchini noodles blanch in the boiling salted water for 2 minutes. Transfer zoodles to a strainer and immediately place under running water to stop cooking. Rinse well and use paper towels to pat dry.

3. Once the tomato mixture is done, toss with zucchini noodles and the avocado. Serve immediately.

Cheesy Zucchini Pasta With Pancetta

Preparation: 20 minutes

Cooking Time: 15 minutes

Serves 4-6

Ingredients:

6 zucchini, spiralized

1 tablespoon olive oil

4 ounce pancetta (Italian bacon), cubed

2 garlic cloves, minced

Handful fresh basil leaves, chopped

Juice and zest of one lemon

4 tablespoons pecorino, grated

Directions:

1. Heat olive oil on medium-high heat in a large pan. Add the pancetta and stir-fry for about 4 to 5 minutes until slightly crisp. Use a slotted spoon to transfer pancetta to a plate.

2. To the same pan, add garlic and sauté for 1-2 minutes or until golden.

3. Add zoodles and sauté for 5 minutes with constant stirring.

4. Stir in lemon juice, zest and pancetta.

5. Transfer to a serving platter and sprinkle with pecorino and chopped basil.

Creamy Spaghetti With Tomato Sauce

Preparation: 20 minutes

Cooking Time: 22 minutes

Serves 5

Ingredients:

5 zucchini squash, spiralized

1 pound ground beef.

3 small leeks, diced

1/2 red onion, diced

1 red bell pepper, thinly sliced

1 14-ounce can artichoke hearts packed in water, quartered

1 tablespoon coconut oil

For The Sauce-

2 tablespoons coconut milk

1 14-ounce can of organic diced tomatoes

2 tablespoons fresh rosemary, minced

1 teaspoon crushed garlic

Sea salt and black pepper to taste

Directions:

1. Heat coconut oil in a wok or large skillet on medium heat. Brown ground beef in hot oil for 5-7 minutes.

2. Add leeks, onion and bell pepper. Cook for about 7 minutes more or until vegetables are tender.

3. In another skillet, combine coconut milk with diced tomatoes (with the juice). Bring to a simmer then stir in rosemary, garlic, salt and pepper.

4. To the wok (with meat and vegetables), add zucchini, artichokes and the sauce. Stir to combine and cook for about 5-6 minutes or until zucchini is al dente

ZUCCHINI RECIPES WITH VEGGIES

Raw Zoodles, Vegetables And Asian Pesto Sauce

Preparation: 20 minutes

Cooking Time: 0 minutes

Serves 4-6

Ingredients:

For the Sauce-

6 tablespoons raw tahini

1 1/2 cups packed cilantro

1 cup walnuts

1 tablespoon sesame oil

1 very small garlic clove

1/2 cup packed basil

Juice of half a lemon

Sea salt and cracked pepper

For the vegetables-

6 medium sized zucchini, spiralized

1/2 cup shiitake mushrooms, sliced very thinly

1 large red bell pepper, sliced very thinly

1 pound asparagus, sliced very thinly

Garnish-

1/2 cup walnuts, crushed

1/4 cup packed cilantro, chopped roughly

1/4 cup green onion, chopped

Sea salt and cracked pepper to taste

Directions:

1. In a food processor, add together tahini, cilantro, walnuts, sesame oil, garlic, basil, lemon juice and water (as needed). Pulse until properly combined.

2. Once the mixture has attained your desired consistency, add salt and pepper as desired then set aside. The sauce thickens if kept in the fridge so you may have to add a little warm water to make it thinner before serving.

3. In a bowl, toss together mushrooms, red bell pepper and asparagus.

4. Toss zucchini noodles with the basil sauce then divide among serving bowls. Top each bowl with vegetable mixture. Garnish with walnuts, cilantro and green onions. Sprinkle with salt and pepper.

Serve immediately.

Zucchini Pasta With Pesto

Preparation: 20 minutes

Cooking Time: 0 minutes

Serves 3-4

Ingredients:

2 large zucchini

1 cup of cherry tomatoes

2/3 cup of roasted garlic walnut pesto

Handful of fresh basil

Sea salt to taste

Directions:

1. Add zucchini noodles to a wire strainer or colander. Add salt liberally and toss to coat. Set aside for 20 minutes to drain. After 20 minutes, rinse well and use paper towels to pat dry.

2. Toss zoodles with the other ingredients until well mixed. Garnish with basil.

Zucchini Pasta With Arugula And Alfredo Sauce

Preparation: 10 minutes

Cooking Time: 0 minutes

Serves 4

Ingredients:

6 zucchini, spiralized

3/4 cup water

3/4 cup cashews (soaked in water for 2 hours)

2 garlic cloves

1/2 teaspoon fresh grated nutmeg

1 tablespoon tahini

1 teaspoon sea salt

1/3 cup fresh squeezed lemon juice,

Black pepper (optional)

3 cups arugula

Directions:

1. Spiralize zucchini. Drain water from cashews and rinse.

2. In a high speed blender, combine 3/4 cup water, cashews, garlic, nutmeg, tahini, sea salt and lemon juice.

Blend on high speed until creamy. Add additional salt and black pepper (if using).

3. Pour the sauce over zucchini noodles and stir in arugula. Serve.

Paleo Raw Pad Thai

Preparation: 20 minutes

Cooking Time: 0 minutes

Serves 2-3

Ingredients:

1 medium zucchini, spiralized

2 large carrots, julienned

1 cup red cabbage, sliced thinly

1 red pepper, sliced thinly

3 green onions, sliced thinly

1 teaspoon sesame seeds

1 tablespoon hemp seeds

For The Dressing -

1/4 cup raw almond butter

1 garlic clove

1 teaspoon freshly grated ginger

2 tablespoons low-sodium tamari

2 tablespoons fresh lime juice

2 1/2 teaspoons maple syrup

2 tablespoons water

1/2 tablespoon toasted sesame oil

Directions:

1. In a large bowl, use your hands to combine zucchini, carrots, cabbage and red pepper.

2. In a bowl, whisk together all the ingredients for the dressing.

3. Place vegetables in serving bowls, top with green onion, sesame seeds and hemp seeds then pour the dressing over all.

Mixed Veggies Ribbon Salad

Preparation: 20 minutes

Cooking Time: 0 minutes

Serves 6

Ingredients:

2 medium zucchini

1 green apple, sliced, diced

4 cup spinach leaves

4 cup kale, torn from the stem

1 tablespoon olive oil

1 tablespoon white balsamic vinegar

1 tablespoon maple syrup

1/2 teaspoon sea salt

Directions:

1. Spiralized the zucchini and place in a large bowl along with diced apple.

2. Roll together spinach and kale leaves (like a burrito) then cut into narrow ribbons. Add to the zucchini bowl.

3. In a small bowl, mix together olive oil, balsamic vinegar, maple syrup and sea salt. Pour this mixture over the bowl of vegetables and mix together. Serve.

Zucchini Fettuccine Alfredo

Preparation: 10 minutes

Cooking Time: 1 hour

Serves 4-6

Ingredients:

3 pounds zucchini, spiralized

1 medium butternut squash

3 tablespoons coconut oil, divided

2 garlic cloves, minced

1 medium yellow onion, chopped

1/2 cup vegetable broth

1 cup full-fat canned coconut milk

2 teaspoons dried rosemary, crushed

1/2 teaspoon sea salt

1 pound shiitake mushrooms, sliced

Freshly-ground black pepper to taste

Directions:

1. Preheat oven to 375F. Grease a baking sheet with about 1 tablespoon of coconut oil.

2. Slice butternut squash in half then place on greased baking sheet, cut side down. Bake for 30-40 minutes or until squash is soft enough to be pierced easily with a fork. Remove from oven and set aside to cool. When squash is cool, scoop out and transfer the flesh to a blender. Discard the skin.

3. Meanwhile, place a skillet on medium heat and add 1 tablespoon of coconut oil to it. Add garlic and onions and sauté for about 3-5 minutes. Transfer to the blender with the butternut squash flesh.

4. Also, add the vegetable broth, coconut milk, rosemary and salt to the blender. Blend until you have a smooth sauce.

5. In a large skillet, heat the remaining 1 tablespoon of coconut oil on medium heat. Sauté mushrooms for 2 minutes or until slightly brown. Add zucchini noodles then cook for 3-4 minutes until al dente. Add the sauce and heat through.

6. Season with black pepper and serve immediately.

Minty Zucchini Pineapple Salad

Preparation: 15 minutes

Cooking Time: 0 minutes

Serves 4

Ingredients:

4 cups of spiralized zucchini

2 cups of pineapple, diced into 1/4-inch chunks

1/2 cup of sliced mint leaves

1 1/2 tablespoons olive oil

1/2 teaspoon sea salt

Juice of 1 lime

Directions:

1. In a large bowl, gently mix together zucchini noodles, pineapple, mint leaves and olive oil.

2. Sprinkle with sea salt and lime juice. Serve immediately.

Zoodles With Creamy Avocado Sauce

Preparation: 10 minutes

Cooking Time: 10 minutes

Serves 3

Ingredients:

3 zucchinis, spiralized

3 carrots, spiralized

1 teaspoon of olive oil

2 avocados

1 packed tablespoon fresh cilantro

1/4 cup sunflower oil

1/4 teaspoon turmeric

1 1/2 teaspoon cumin

Juice of 1 lemon

Salt and pepper, to taste

Directions:

1. In a skillet, add 1 teaspoon of olive oil and sauté carrots for 1 minute.

2. Add zucchini and continue cooking for 5-6 minutes until vegetables are soft. Remove vegetables from heat and transfer to a colander to drain.

3. Meanwhile, in a blender, combine avocados, cilantro, sunflower oil, turmeric, cumin, lemon juice, salt and pepper. Puree until smooth and creamy.

4. Pour sauce on vegetable noodles and serve.

CUCUMBER RECIPES

Cucumber Noodles With Ginger, Asparagus And Sesame Sauce

Preparation: 25 minutes

Cooking Time: 0 minutes

Serves 3

Ingredients:

2 small green onions (scallions), sliced thinly

1 2-inch piece of fresh ginger, peeled, grated finely

2 tablespoons light olive oil

1 teaspoon toasted sesame oil

1 1/2 tablespoons of coconut aminos

Dash of red pepper flakes

Sea salt, to taste

2 English cucumbers, peeled

1 bunch asparagus, ends trimmed and sliced into 2 inch pieces on the diagonal

2 tablespoons of toasted sesame (optional garnish)

Directions:

1. In a large bowl, combine the green onions, ginger, olive oil, sesame oil, coconut aminos and red pepper flakes. Whisk together then add a little salt to taste. Set aside.

2. Slice the cucumbers and asparagus into noodles.

3. Add water and salt to a large pot. Bring to boil over high heat then add asparagus noodles. Let the asparagus noodles blanch in the boiling salted water for 2 minutes. Transfer asparagus noodles to a strainer and immediately place under running water to stop cooking. Drain.

4. Add cucumber noodles and cooled blanched asparagus to the green onion sauce. Toss to combine. Serve, sprinkled with toasted sesame seeds.

Cucumber And Mango Salad

Preparation: 15 minutes

Cooking Time: 0 minutes

Serves 6

Ingredients:

1 seedless cucumber, unpeeled, sliced very thin

3 mangoes, peeled, diced into 1-inch pieces

1/4 cup chopped fresh cilantro

1 small red onion, sliced very thin

2 teaspoon lemon-flavored olive oil

2 tablespoon lemon juice

1/2 teaspoon salt

1/2 teaspoon black pepper

Directions:

1. Combine all the ingredients in a serving bowl.

2. Place in the fridge for about 1 hour. Serve chilled.

Black pepper, to taste

3/4 cup marinara sauce

Fresh chopped parsley

Directions:

1. Add oil to a pan on medium heat. Add onion and sauté for about 2 minutes.

2. Add basil, mushrooms, salt and pepper then cook for 5 minutes or until water from the mushroom has reduced.

3. Add carrot noodles and sty-fry for just one minute.

4. Stir in marinara sauce and let simmer for about 7-8 minutes.

5. Top with parsley and serve.

Carrot Spaghetti With Creamy Garlic Sauce

Preparation: 10 minutes

Cooking Time: 5 minutes

Serves 1

Ingredients:

1 big carrot, spiralized

1 tablespoon olive oil

1 tablespoon tahini

1 teaspoon tamari

3 tablespoon fresh lemon juice

1 small garlic clove, grated

1 teaspoon grated ginger

Toppings: sesame seeds, handful of chopped parsley, pine nuts

Directions:

1. Cut carrot into noodles.

2. In a bowl, mix together olive oil, tahini, tamari, lemon juice, garlic and ginger.

3. Combine sauce with carrot noodles, mixing gently with your hands.

4. Top with sesame seeds, parsley and pine nuts. Serve.

Zesty Carrot Noodles with Ginger Almond Sauce

Preparation: 15 minutes

Cooking Time: 0 minutes

Serves 4-6

Ingredients:

5 large carrots, peeled, spiralized

4 tablespoons coconut milk

2 tablespoons creamy almond butter

2 tablespoons liquid aminos

1 tablespoon fresh ginger, peeled, grated

2 large garlic cloves, chopped finely

1 tablespoon lime juice

Pinch cayenne pepper

Kosher salt to taste

2 tablespoons fresh cilantro, chopped finely

1/3 cup roasted cashews

Directions:

1. To make the sauce: Combine coconut milk, almond butter, aminos, ginger, garlic, cayenne pepper, lime juice and salt. Mix until creamy and smooth.

2. Place carrot noodles in a serving bowl. Pour the ginger almond sauce on top then toss to combine. Serve garnished with cilantro and roasted cashews.

Carrot Noodles With Cauliflower Cream Sauce

Preparation: 10 minutes

Cooking Time: 20 minutes

Serves 3

Ingredients:

4 cups spiralized carrots

1 head broccoli, stems chopped off

1 head purple cauliflower

1/4 cup unsweetened almond milk

1/8 cup coconut milk

1/8 cup nutritional yeast

1/4 teaspoon sea salt

1 teaspoon cumin

Directions:

1. Add 5 cups of water to a pot and bring to a boil. Cut off the cauliflower stems and break cauliflower apart. Add to the boiling water and let simmer for about 10 minutes.

2. Transfer cauliflower to a strainer to drain then place in a blender. Add the almond milk, coconut milk, nutritional yeast, sea salt and cumin. Blend until smooth and creamy.

3. Bring another 6 cups of water to a boil. Add carrot noodles to boiling water and let simmer for about 3 minutes. Add the broccoli and simmer for another 3 minutes. Drain.

4. Pour the sauce over carrots and broccoli. Serve garnished with parsley.

Carrot Rice With Bacon

Preparation: 15 minutes

Cooking Time: 15 minutes

Serves 2

Ingredients:

Cooking spray

4 carrots, peeled, spiralized

4 slices of center cut bacon

1 cup of sliced green onions

2 teaspoons minced garlic

2 tablespoon fresh lemon juice

1 cup + 2 tablespoons low-sodium vegetable broth

Pepper, to taste

2 teaspoons freshly chopped parsley

Directions:

1. Coat a skillet with cooking spray and place on medium heat. Add bacon slices and cook for about 5 minutes or until crispy. Remove bacon with a slotted spoon and set aside on a plate lined with paper towels. Dice bacon slices when cool.

2. Place carrot noodles in a food processor. Pulse for just about 5-10 seconds to break noodles into rice-like bits. Set aside.

3. To the skillet (with bacon grease), add green onions and garlic. Stir-fry for 1 minute then stir in lemon juice and 2 tablespoons vegetable broth. Season

with pepper then stir in carrot rice. Let cook for about 1 minute then add the remaining vegetable broth. Cook until the liquid is completely absorbed.

4. When the carrot rice is done, gently stir in the diced bacon. Serve, topped with parsley.

SWEET POTATO RECIPES WITH MEAT, SEAFOOD OR EGGS

Sweet Potato Spaghetti With Prosciutto And Figs

Preparation: 10 minutes

Cooking Time: 20 minutes

Serves 4

Ingredients:

2 large sweet potatoes

1 cup dried figs, diced roughly

1 4-ounce package prosciutto, cut into 1 inch squares

1 cup slivered almonds

1/2 teaspoon sea salt

1/2 tablespoon olive oil

2 tablespoons water

Directions:

1. Wash sweet potatoes, peel and spiralize. Dice the dried figs and remove hard stems. Cut prosciutto into 1 inch squares.

2. Add olive oil to a large skillet over medium heat. Add sweet potato noodles and sea salt. Cook with frequent stirring for about 5-7 minutes or until potato noodles are tender. Transfer to a plate

3. In the same pan over medium heat, add the sliced prosciutto and cook for 1-2 minutes on each side. Add figs and almonds then cook, stirring often for 3 minutes, more or until figs are soft and light brown.

4. Stir in the sweet potato noodles and let heat through. Serve immediately.

Sweet Potato Pasta With Buffalo Chicken Alfredo

Preparation: 15 minutes

Cooking Time: 20 minutes

Serves 4

Ingredients:

1 pound of chicken

2-3 tablespoons olive oil

3 sweet potatoes, spiralized

1 tablespoon nondairy butter

1 cup heavy coconut cream

2 tablespoon hot sauce

4 teaspoon starch (arrowroot or tapioca)

1/4 teaspoon garlic powder

Salt and pepper to taste

Directions:

1. In a saucepan, combine butter, coconut cream, hot sauce, starch, garlic powder, salt and pepper. Heat with continuous stirring until thickened. Set aside.

2. Add some olive oil to a large skillet on medium-high heat. Season chicken with salt and pepper then cook in hot oil until browned. Transfer to a plate, let cool and cut to pieces.

3. Spiralize the sweet potatoes. Add more olive oil to the skillet on medium heat and cook sweet potato noodles until done.

4. Combine noodles with chicken and sauce.

Crispy Sweet Potato Noodles With Meatballs

Preparation: 15 minutes

Cooking Time: 35minutes

Serves 4

Ingredients:

3 tablespoons ghee

1/2 yellow onion, minced

1 teaspoon grated ginger

3 garlic cloves, minced

3 sweet potatoes

2 pounds ground beef

1/2 teaspoon sea salt

1/4 cup coconut aminos

1 orange, juiced

Directions:

1. Melt 1 tablespoon ghee in a skillet on medium heat. Add the onion and stir-fry for about 7-8 minutes, or until translucent. Add the ginger and garlic and cook for 1 minute. Remove from heat and transfer to a bowl to cool.

2. Spiralize the sweet potatoes. Add more ghee to the skillet on medium heat and cook sweet potato noodles until done. Remove from heat and set aside.

3. In a large bowl, combine the cool onion mixture with ground beef, salt and thyme. Mix gently with your hands and form into about 20, 1-1/2" meatballs.

3. Melt the remaining ghee in the skillet on medium heat. Brown meatballs 3 minutes on one side. Flip meatballs then add coconut aminos and orange

juice. Cover and cook for about 10 minutes. Remove meatballs from the skillet and set aside.

4. Leave the remaining juices in the skillet and turn up to medium-high heat. Heat for about 5-10 minutes until the liquid thickens.

5. Serve sweet potato noodles with meatballs and sauce.

Sweet Potato Noodle Waffles

Preparation: 5 minutes

Cooking Time: 20 minutes

Serves 1

Ingredients:

1 medium sweet potato, peeled, spiralized

1 teaspoon pumpkin spice

1/2 teaspoon ground cinnamon

1/4 teaspoon ground ginger

1/4 teaspoon ground nutmeg

1/4 teaspoon allspice

1 medium egg, beaten

Cooking spray

1 tablespoon maple syrup

Directions:

1. Heat up your waffle iron.

2. Coat a large skillet with cooking spray and place on medium heat. Add the sweet potato noodles and cook with frequent turning for about 10 minutes.

3. Transfer cooked noodles to a bowl, add the spices and mix well.

4. Add the beaten egg and toss to combine.

5. Spray some cooking spray on the waffle iron. Pack the noodles into the waffle iron.

6. Cook according to the settings of the iron. Serve with maple syrup.

Directions:

1. Peel butternut squash, slice off ends then spiralize.

2. In a food processor, combine pomegranates and oranges. Chop into fine pieces.

3. Mix noodles with the other ingredients and serve.

Raw Butternut Squash Pasta With Sun-Dried Tomato Sauce

Preparation: 15 minutes

Cooking Time: 0 minutes

Serves 4

Ingredients:

2 fresh butternut squash, peeled, spiralized

1/2 cup sun dried tomatoes

4 medium fresh organic tomatoes

1 teaspoon dried herbs de Provence

2 fresh garlic cloves

Juice of 1 lemon

1/2 teaspoon sea salt

1/4 teaspoon ground pepper

1/2 cup avocado oil

Directions:

1. In a large food processor bowl, combine sun dried tomatoes, fresh tomatoes, dried herbs, garlic, lemon juice, salt and pepper.

2. Process for 30 seconds on high. Scrape down the sides, add avocado oil then process for about 1 minute more or until smooth and creamy.

3. Toss sauce with butternut squash noodles.

Butternut Squash Pasta With Sage

Preparation: 10 minutes

Cooking Time: 10 minutes

Serves 4

Ingredients:

4 cups spiralized butternut squash

2 teaspoons extra virgin olive oil

4 tablespoons ghee

10 medium fresh sage leaves

Salt and pepper to taste

Directions:

1. Preheat your oven to 400F. Line a large baking sheet with parchment paper.

2. Arrange butternut squash noodles on the parchment paper, drizzle with olive oil and toss gently to coat.

3. Bake for about 7 minutes and remove from oven.

4. Meanwhile, melt ghee in a large skillet on medium heat. Add sage and sauté for about 2-3 minutes until darken and fragrant. Remove from heat. Toss with butternut squash and serve immediately.

Butternut Squash Pasta With Kale

Preparation: 15 minutes

Cooking Time: 15 minutes

Serves 2

Ingredients:

1 medium butternut squash, spiralized

1/2 teaspoon nutmeg

2 tablespoons of fresh sage, chopped finely

6 tablespoons ghee

3 cups dino kale, ribs removed, leaves ripped into 1-inch pieces

1/4 cup pine nuts, toasted

Directions:

1. Preheat your oven to 400F. Line a large baking sheet with parchment paper.

2. Lay butternut squash noodles on the parchment paper and bake for about 7 minutes.

3. Meanwhile, melt ghee in a large skillet on medium heat. Add nutmeg and sage then cook with frequent stirring until browned. Set aside.

4. In the same skillet, add kale and sauté for about 4-5 minutes or until it softens.

5. In a large bowl, combine butternut squash noodles, kale with ghee, sage and pine nuts. Toss to combine then serve.

Butternut Squash Noodles With Spinach And Bacon

Preparation: 15 minutes

Cooking Time: 20 minutes

Serves 2

Ingredients:

1 butternut squash, spiralized

1 tablespoon extra virgin olive oil

Kosher salt to taste

Freshly ground black pepper to taste

4 slices thick bacon, sliced into small strips

1 onion, sliced thinly

3 garlic cloves, minced

2 cups fresh spinach, chopped roughly

1/4 cup chicken broth

Directions:

1. Preheat oven to 400F. Line a baking sheet with parchment paper.

2. Toss butternut squash noodles with olive oil, salt and pepper. Place the noodles on baking sheet and roast for about 10 minutes.

3. Meanwhile, add bacon to a large skillet on medium high heat and cook until crisp about 5 minutes. Transfer bacon to a plate lined with paper towel. Reserve just 2 tablespoon of bacon grease.

4. Return skillet (with bacon grease) to medium heat. Add onion and sauté for about 2 minutes, or until lightly brown, then stir in the garlic. Add the roasted butternut squash noodles and toss.

5. Reduce to low heat then add spinach and chicken broth. Stir to combine.

6. Serve butternut squash noodles with bacon.

1 teaspoon red chili flakes

1 cup diced tomatoes

1/4 teaspoon salt

Handful of flat-leaf parsley

Black pepper to taste

Directions:

1. Melt coconut oil in a large skillet on medium heat. Add parsnip noodles and cook for about 20 minutes or until softened. Set aside in a plate.

2. Add garlic and onion to the skillet and cook until soft.

3. Stir in anchovies, capers and olives. Add chili flakes, tomatoes and salt then stir to combine.

4. Sprinkle with black pepper, garnish with fresh parsley and serve at once.

Easy Parsnip Spaghetti

Preparation: 15 minutes

Cooking Time: 10 minutes

Serves 4

Ingredients:

4 medium parsnips, spiralized

2 tablespoons ghee

1/2 teaspoon grated fresh ginger

1/2 onion, sliced

1 garlic clove, minced

1 tablespoons coconut aminos

1 tablespoon fresh lime juice

Pinch of salt

Pinch teaspoon cayenne pepper

Directions:

1. Add ghee to a skillet on medium heat. Stir-fry parsnips for 5-10 minutes or until golden and crispy. Remove from oil and set aside.

2. To the skillet, add ginger, garlic and onion then stir-fry for 30 seconds.

3. Add the remaining ingredients and heat through.

4. Remove sauce from heat and toss with parsnip noodle.

Parsnip Noodles With Bolognese Sauce

Preparation: 10 minutes

Cooking Time: 50 minutes

Serves 4

Ingredients:

4 parsnips, peeled, spiralized

2 tablespoons of lemon juice

1 tablespoon of lard

For The Sauce -

1 tablespoon of lard

1 medium onion, chopped

2 celery stalks, thinly sliced

4 ounces of pancetta, chopped

1 pound of grass-fed ground beef

4 carrots, shredded

2 cups of beef broth

1/2 cup of red wine

1 can of full fat coconut milk

1 can of tomato sauce

2 bay leaves

1/2 teaspoon of fennel seed

1 teaspoon of black pepper

Directions:

1. Toss parsnip noodles with lemon juice.

2. Add 1 tablespoon of lard to a skillet on medium high heat. Stir fry the parsnips for about 2-3 minutes or until soft and lightly golden. Transfer to a plate and set aside.

3. Return the skillet to medium heat and add another 1 tablespoon of lard. Add onion and celery and sauté until onions are soft.

4. Add pancetta and beef and cook until brown. Stir in the carrots.

5. Add broth, red wine, coconut milk, tomato sauce, bay leaves, fennel seed and pepper. Stir and bring to a boil.

6. Reduce to medium low heat and let simmer for 30-40 minutes with occasional stirring. Serve parsnip noodles with the sauce.

OTHER VEGETABLES AND FRUITS RECIPES

Yellow Squash Pad Thai

Preparation: 20 minutes

Cooking Time: 15minutes

Serves 6

Ingredients:

For The Sauce-

1/3 cup water

1/3 cup lime juice

1 tablespoon coconut vinegar

3 tablespoons fish sauce

2 tablespoons raw honey

4 tablespoons palm shortening, divided

1/4 teaspoon cayenne or to taste

For The Stir-Fry-

1/4 teaspoon sea salt

2 large eggs

12 ounces medium shrimp, peeled, deveined

1 medium shallot, minced

3 cloves garlic, minced

8 yellow squash, spiralized

Garlic Lemon Broccoli Noodle With Bacon

Preparation: 15 minutes

Cooking Time: 25 minutes

Serves 4

Ingredients:

3 large heads broccoli, spiralized

6 slices bacon

Cooking spray

2 tablespoons of olive oil

1/4 teaspoon of red-pepper flakes

Salt and pepper to taste

5 medium garlic cloves, thinly sliced

Zest of 1/2 of a lemon

Juice of 1 lemon

3 tablespoons nutritional yeast

Directions:

1. Blanch broccoli noodles for 2 to 3 minutes in salted boiling water. Drain and dry with paper towels.

2. Coat a large skillet with cooking spray and place on medium heat. Add bacon slices to the pan and cook for about 3 minutes on each side or until brown and crisp. Transfer to a plate lined with paper towel. Crumble when cool.

3. Wipe out the skillet, add olive oil and return to medium heat. When the oil is hot, add broccoli noodles, red-pepper flakes, salt and pepper. Cook for 2 minutes with occasional stirring.

4. Add lemon juice, zest, garlic and nutritional yeast. Cover and cook for about 5 minutes more or until the broccoli is lightly browned.

5. Remove from heat then stir in the bacon. Serve immediately.

Broccoli-Carrot Slaw With Sunflower Seeds And Dried Cranberries

Preparation: 15 minutes

Cooking Time: 0 minutes

Serves 4

Ingredients:

2 cups spiralized carrots

2 cups spiralized broccoli stem

1/4 cup green onions, thinly sliced

1/2 cup dried cranberries

1/2 cup sunflower seed kernels

For The Dressing -

1 1/2 tablespoon freshly squeezed lemon juice

1/3 cup homemade paleo mayonnaise

1 tablespoon honey

1 tablespoon rice vinegar

1/2 teaspoon kosher salt

Directions:

1. Combine all ingredients (lemon juice, mayonnaise, honey, rice vinegar and salt) for the dressing in a small bowl. Whisk well to incorporate.

2. In a large bowl, combine the carrot noodles, broccoli noodles, green onions and cranberries

3. Pour the dressing on the vegetable noodles and toss to coat. Place in the fridge for a few hours to chill.

4. Toss with sunflower seeds when you want to serve.

Creamy Eggplant Noodles

Preparation: 20 minutes

Cooking Time: 30 minutes

Serves 3

Ingredients:

1 eggplant, peeled, spiralized

Olive oil

1/2 cup almond cream cheese

1 cup homemade marinara sauce

Salt to taste

Directions:

1. Soak eggplant in a large bowl of salted water for about 15-20 minutes. Drain.

2. Meanwhile, make your homemade marinara sauce.

3. Heat oil in a skillet, add the eggplant noodles and cook, tossing occasionally until translucent.

4. Add almond cream cheese, marinara sauce and salt to taste.

Eggplant Pasta Bolognaise

Preparation: 15 minutes

Cooking Time: 30 minutes

Serves 2

Ingredients:

3 large eggplants, peeled and spiralized

1 pound minced beef

1 large onion, peeled, diced

2 garlic cloves, minced

1 large tomato, seeded, diced

1 tablespoon of tomato paste

2 cups of tomato sauce

Olive oil

Salt and pepper to taste

Directions:

1. In a large pan, add a few tablespoon of olive oil to coat the surface. Sauté garlic and onion until onions are slightly brown.

2. Add the minced meat then cook until browned.

3. Stir in diced tomato, tomato paste, tomato sauce, salt and pepper. Let it simmer for several minutes. Add a little water if you want a thinner sauce.

4. Meanwhile, add a little olive oil to another pan. Add eggplant noodles and stir fry until cooked.

5. Divide the cooked eggplant into two bowls then top each bowl with the bolognaise sauce.

Daikon Noodles With Spinach And Red Cabbage Slaw

Preparation: 20 minutes

Cooking Time: 0 minutes

Serves 4

Ingredients:

4 large Daikon radishes, peeled, spiralized

1/2 large head of red cabbage, sliced thinly

4 ounce of baby spinach, sliced thinly

2 teaspoons toasted sesame oil

2 tablespoons extra virgin olive oil

1 teaspoon maple syrup

1 1/2 tablespoon apple cider vinegar

2 teaspoons Dijon mustard

Pinch of sea salt

Pinch of freshly ground black pepper

2 tablespoons black and white sesame seeds

Directions:

1. In a large serving bowl, whisk together sesame oil, olive oil, maple syrup, apple cider vinegar, Dijon mustard, salt and pepper.

2. Add daikon noodles, red cabbage and spinach, to the dressing then toss to combine.

3. Add sesame seeds then let sit for at least 10 minutes before serving.

Paleo Daikon "Fried Rice"

Preparation: 20 minutes

Cooking Time: 0 minutes

Serves 1

Ingredients:

1 1/2 cups "riced" daikon

1 1/2 tablespoons sesame oil

1 tablespoon ghee

1/4 cup carrots, diced

1/4 teaspoon fresh ginger

1 garlic clove, crushed

2 tablespoons coconut aminos

1/4 teaspoon crushed red pepper

1 egg

Directions:

1. Peel the daikon radish and spiralize. Use a knife to chop spirals into "rice" pieces.

2. Add sesame oil to a large skillet on medium heat. Add daikon rice and sauté with constant stirring for 5-7 minutes.

3. Stir in ghee, carrots, ginger, garlic, coconut aminos and red pepper.

4. Crack the egg over the pan and stir it into the fried rice. Cook until the daikon rice is crispy. Taste then add salt and pepper as needed. Serve immediately.

Jicama Fries With Sesame Ginger Sauce

Preparation: 10 minutes

Cooking Time: 5 minutes

Serves 5

Ingredients:

1 large jicama, peeled, spiralized

2 tablespoons toasted sesame oil

1/2 teaspoon grated fresh ginger

1/2 onion, sliced

1 garlic clove, minced

2 tablespoons coconut aminos

1 tablespoon apple cider vinegar

Salt to taste

2 teaspoon cayenne pepper

Sesame seeds, raw – for garnish)

Directions:

1. Use a knife to chop jicama spirals into short noodles.

2. Add sesame oil to a skillet on medium-high heat. Add ginger, garlic and onion then stir-fry for 30 seconds.

3. Add jicama and stir-fry for 2 minutes.

4. Add aminos, apple cider vinegar, salt and cayenne pepper. Stir together and let heat through.

5. Garnish with sesame seeds and serve.

Crispy Jicama With Ginger Almond Butter Sauce

Preparation: 20 minutes

Cooking Time: 0 minutes

Serves 5

Ingredients:

1 large jicama, peeled, spiralized

1 tablespoon olive oil

1/2 teaspoon grated fresh ginger

1/2 onion, sliced

1 garlic clove, minced

1 tablespoons coconut aminos

1 tablespoon fresh lime juice

Pinch of salt

Pinch teaspoon cayenne pepper

Directions:

1. Use a knife to chop jicama spirals into short noodles.

2. Add oil to a skillet on medium-high heat. Add ginger, garlic and onion then stir-fry for 30 seconds.

3. Add jicama and stir-fry for 2 minutes.

4. Add almond butter, broth, coconut aminos, lime juice, salt and pepper. Stir together and let heat through.

Serve immediately.

END

Thank you for reading my book. If you enjoyed it, won't you please take a moment to leave a good review at your retailer?

Thanks!

Paula Corey

51246386R00066

Made in the USA
Lexington, KY
17 April 2016